Campus Crusade for Chris

A
Devotional Interpretation
of
Familiar Hymns

BY

EARL E. BROCK

Essay Index Reprint Series

BOOKS FOR LIBRARIES PRESS
FREEPORT, NEW YORK

STANDARD BOOK NUMBER:

8369-1395-7

LIBRARY OF CONGRESS CATALOG CARD NUMBER:

72-93319

PRINTED IN THE UNITED STATES OF AMERICA

Foreword

Too often men sing because they like the sound of a song rather than because they appreciate its thought. A missionary visiting a tribe whose language he did not speak found them singing with great spirit and seemingly with profound enjoyment. Being especially interested in music and its expression as it is carried over from one language to another, he asked one of the leaders what the song actually meant in their tongue. The man hesitated. The missionary asked again and pointed to the words of a particular stanza. The man looked, and still was puzzled. "I am surprised," he said. "Those words do not mean anything. We must have been singing them because we liked the sound."

A song should be more than mere words musically uttered. There must be a heart touch before it can touch another heart. To appreciate it fully one needs to put himself as nearly as possible in the place of the author to interpret his mood and to grasp the spiritual application that must have been in his soul.

Naturally, interpretations differ. One man looking at a painting sees a rippling lake; another, the swaying trees along the shore. Likewise, one man looking into a song may find a challenge; another, may see a prayer. Whether the interpretation be a call to higher service or an expression of devotion, it gives to the hymn a deeper meaning and makes it dearer to the heart. In the dawning understanding there is a depth of vision and a new grasp of the message God has for man.

It is with this in mind that these studies are passed on—the hope that their interpretations may help others see spiritual significance that has not been evident before—the prayer that they may give a greater appreciation of Him in whose name we sing.

E. E. B.

Boulder, Colo.

4

Contents

1

"When I Survey the Wondrous Cross"

WE HAVE become so accustomed to thinking of our great English hymns as songs for the ages that it is hard to realize that even the oldest of them were given to us only a little over two centuries ago. Before that it had been the custom to sing nothing in the church services except metrical versions of the Psalms, for it was claimed that the Psalms were inspired to serve as a hymn book for all generations.

There had been a few English hymn writers, but they had been so few that no standard or precedent had been established. So small was their number and so poorly defined was their position that James Montgomery speaks of Isaac Watts as the inventor of hymns in our language.

In 1707, while still a young man, Watts published a volume of *Hymns and Spiritual Songs* in which each hymn was of his own composition. Along with this, he printed an essay denying that the Psalms were intended to be used as the sole hymnal for all time. He argued that it was the duty of the church to produce new songs that would express the Christian faith as the Psalms had expressed the Jewish.

"When I Survey the Wondrous Cross", one of the two

hundred and ten in that first edition, is not only the best of Watts' productions; it is one of the greatest spiritual songs in our language. If we are to judge by the number of hymnals in which it is contained, common consent places it among the very greatest, for it is said that there is only one other used more extensively. That is "Rock of Ages."

There is a challenge in the opening words:

> "When I survey the wondrous cross,
>   On which the Prince of glory died,
> My richest gain I count but loss,
>   And pour contempt on all my pride."

It is said that our hymns have never had a severer critic than Matthew Arnold. On the last day of his life this song was sung in the services of the Sefton Park Presbyterian church in Liverpool, which he attended. As he came down to lunch he was heard softly repeating the opening lines. During the course of the luncheon he spoke of it as the greatest hymn in the language.

It is not surprising that he pondered musingly over the opening words of the song. There is a heart touch in the vision of the cross that brings to man a knowledge of the divine. Even the hardened centurion, whose soldiers only a short time before had cast lots for the prize garment among those of the condemned, came under the spell of its magic influence. This leader of men, accustomed to facing death without hesitation, was filled with horror. "Surely," he cried as the divine revelation came to him, "This was the Son of God."

With horror his thoughts turned to the fact that they had killed the friend who came to help and save. With wonder in his heart he must have asked, "Surely the Son of God did not have to die. How could He let them crucify Him? How could He do it?" With just as great wonder in our hearts we ask the same question today. The cross was the most cruel instrument of death the Roman could devise. Its shame was greater even than the shame of the gallows or the electric chair. As its vision brings to us a picture of the supreme greatness of God's love, with hushed voices we too can only ask, "How could He do it?"

No experience in life has given us the ability to measure the love that gave itself on Calvary's tree. We can measure it only as we measure God Himself. But as there comes some knowledge of this wondrous manifestation to our heart we stand in awe before its greatness. No experience of ours has brought us to such a point. Our hearts have known the meaning of love and sacrifice but not such love and sacrifice as this. When we stand in the presence of Him who gave Himself for us no heart experience or sacrifice seems meet even to compare with His.

With hearts that respond in a great throb of love we can only cry:

"Forbid it, Lord! that I should boast
Save in the death of Christ, my God;
All the vain things that charm me most
I sacrifice them to His blood."

A similar cry came from the great apostle. The Galatians were losing sight of the Christ and of the cross. Teachers had come among them laying emphasis on ceremonial observances and already they were beginning to drift back towards formal Judaism. They were beginning to take pride in the ceremonies they performed and the works they did. "O foolish Galatians," he cried, "who hath bewitched you?" He spoke emphatically, for he knew well that the primary need of Christian life is a vision that looks not to self but to Christ.

Paul had known what it was to boast. In those fanatical earlier days it must have given him great satisfaction to know that among the persecuted Christians there was no name so feared as was the name of Saul of Tarsus. In his Christian life he came to a position even higher, for he labored more abundantly than they all. In this he did not glory, save as it gave an opportunity for greater service. He had caught sight of the cross, and compared with the great outpouring of God's love his own achievements seemed so small that with hushed breath he could only pray, "God forbid that I should glory, save in the cross of our Lord Jesus Christ."

The soldier back of the firing line is proud of the uniform he wears, but as the bleeding hero of the charge is carried by, he stands speechless in the presence of one who has given so much more than he. We may be proud of the things with which God has blessed us—proud of the deeds He has helped us to accomplish, but with the vision of the cross before us we stand silent and filled with awe. We recognize the presence of the great giver and what can we say of our puny achievements when

> "See, from His head, His hands, His feet,
> Sorrow and love flow mingled down;
> Did e'er such love and sorrow meet,
> Or thorns compose so rich a crown?"

As in the sympathy of His great heart He wept with the sisters of Bethany, the assembled friends thought of the dead brother and said, "How He must have loved him!" Today as there comes to us a vision of the darkened cross on Calvary our hearts are filled with awe. "Oh," we whisper, "how He must have loved us!" We have heard from childhood that "God so loved the world," but it did not seem like this. That face, pale and drawn with suffering—the clots of half-dry blood where mocking soldiers had pressed the thorns—the life slowly ebbing away—and for us!

As we stand humbled before Him the whisper seems drawn from those suffering lips:

"I gave, I gave my life for thee,
What hast thou given me?"

and almost of themselves our lips begin to move with the only answer that is fitting—the closing stanza of the old hymn:

"Were the whole realm of nature mine,
    That were a present far too small:
Love so amazing, so divine,
    Demands my soul, my life, my all."

Nothing else is fitting. If we are to be His followers we must give as He gave—not a part of our possessions or a tithe of our time but ourselves—our all. He held back nothing from us; we cannot meet the challenge of His cross and hold back any thing from Him.

2

"O Love That Wilt Not Let Me Go"

THERE are few of us who have not had a little child creep into our arms as if trying to hide while its whole body shook with sobs and its childish burden seemed too heavy to bear. Often, too, our hearts were burdened with a realization that even though we called those troubles childish we could do but little to remove them from the path of our child.

Quite likely it is well that we could not. In the mistaken drive of an overzealous love we might have taken from him the very experiences that made him strong. When he fled to us he was not thinking of their removal. His heart was too burdened for that. He was not seeking advice, a word of cheer, or a bit of help in a difficult task. What he needed was comfort.

As with trembling soul he clung tightly to what seemed his only refuge his sobs began to cease. It was not because of what we said or did. His heart was too burdened to hear more than the murmur of our voice. With head thrust behind our arm, he could neither see nor know what we did, save as he felt the touch of a loving hand. It was this that checked his sobs. The burden was just as real in his world, but the touch of love had taken away its sting. As he clung to one who understood, and felt the warmth of encircling arms, the grief of his heart was stilled. The troubles were still there but he had found something greater than they. He had found a love that would not let him go.

It must have been some such experience that stirred the soul of George Matheson. We know by his own acknowledgement that there was a heart-burden that seemed too heavy to bear. No friends or companions were at hand, which probably was well. There was no human heart to whom he could go—nowhere to turn except to Him who understands. But he had God. That was sufficient.

Like a child, he turned to the only arms available and in the warmth of their clasp he found a soothing for his sorrow. Then, along with the comfort of the encircling arms, there came a realization of the divine presence. When the first paroxysm of grief had passed so that he could hear, God spoke to him in the words of this song. Matheson seemed to realize this, for in speaking of the writing of it he said, "It was the quickest bit of work I ever did in my life. I had the impression rather of having it dictated to me by some inward voice than of working it out by myself." He knew that he must continue to face the bitter experience. Like Paul's thorn in the flesh, it could not be removed, but God had given him the answer. He had reached out with a comforting touch of understanding love and had taught him to sing:

> "O Love that wilt not let me go,
> I rest my weary soul in Thee:
> I give Thee back the life I owe,
> That in Thine ocean depths its flow
> May richer, fuller be."

Those who would know the full extent of a love that will not let one go need only to study the life of Judas. It is not hard to see how Jesus would hold on to men like James and John. They might be overly harsh in some of their dealings with their fellow men, but their severity grew out of a mistaken loyalty to their Lord. It is not hard to see how He would hold on to Peter, rash and impulsive as Peter was. He might need rebuke but there was no question of his love. He might make his boasts and then in weakness fail in the hour of trial, but on the dark night of the betrayal his was the only hand raised in defense of his Master. Peter knew that one man could not withstand that multitude. Probably his only thought was that while he gave his life to hold them for a moment his Master could slip away in the shadows of the garden. Mistaken in his understanding? Yes, but willing to die, as he thought, to save the life of Him whom he loved. Whatever their failures may have been, the eleven loved Jesus and He knew it. There could be no doubt of this, for every one of them had knowingly risked his life in coming to Jerusalem with Him.

With Judas it was different. Jesus had known that there was no real love there. He had known that Judas was not honest in his dealings with those who trusted him. Jesus knew that Judas was planning to betray Him and still He held on to him. The heart of the Master could not bear to let even a traitor go, so long as there was one ray of hope.

It would have been easier to have warned the others after Judas left, but Jesus spoke of it while they were all together. He knew that the man who sees his plan discovered will sometimes desist, and in the greatness of a love that did not want to let anyone go He was trying to give Judas another chance.

Even though man in his frequent critical spirit looks at the evident failures and blames the best of the disciples, the Son of man, in the greatness of His heart, held on to the worst, so as long as that man would give Him a chance.

It is not surprising that Matheson came to the decision expressed in the first two verses:

> "O Love that wilt not let me go
> I rest my weary soul in Thee."

It is the natural response for one who has caught sight of God's love. Man cannot truly read John 3:16 without knowing that God cares. He cannot ponder its message without coming to the realization that one who cares so much will never fail him in the problems of life. The transformation of the eleven is proof of His power. The extent of a love that does not want to let anyone go is measured in the case of the disciple who would not respond. The man who knows these things knows that he can trust God and not be afraid.

The song is not broken up into separate and distinct parts. It is a harmonious whole. The stanzas do not have separate themes, as might seem at a casual examination. The love, the light, the joy and the cross that stand out so prominently in the separate stanzas are all bound together into one great expression of trust. The key is found in the opening line. When one grasps this central theme, the others fall into line to complete the thought of a love that will not let one go.

Matheson had not learned why he had to suffer, but he had learned that he could depend on God's love. His failure to understand did not seem so great after all. God knew and God cared. That was enough. With the light of faith he could see that all was well, and sing:

> "O Light that followest all my way,
> I yield my flick'ring torch to Thee:
> My heart restores its borrowed ray,
> That in Thy sunshine's blaze its day
> May brighter, fairer be."

God had a greater message for him. He closed the second stanza with the thought that as his life came more completely into the light of God's knowledge he might be able to understand. He had not yet realized that when God touches the soul it can smile through its tears. He had thought that there might be a brighter day, but he had failed to see that God's love shining through the clouds of the darkest day can bring a rainbow for the soul.

When such a thought began to dawn upon him he could scarcely believe it. He could not see how it was possible for one with all the burden of his heart to find joy unless the burden were removed. God spoke again. He began to understand, and his understanding found expression in his song:

> "O Joy that seekest me through pain,
> I cannot close my heart to Thee:
> I trace the rainbow through the rain,
> And feel the promise is not vain
> That morn shall tearless be."

His thoughts turned to the burden of his heart. Like a little child, he had fled to the Father. Clinging tightly and with heart too burdened to speak, he had felt the warmth of loving arms that would not let him go, and had found comfort. He had wondered why he had to suffer, and God had answered, "If you knew the greatness of my love you would know that if it were best I would take the burden away. Trust me. My love is great and my knowledge greater than thine." Matheson had longed for a life untouched by sorrow, and God had given him a joy triumphant over pain. He had prayed that the load might be lifted from his shoulders, and God had given him strength that he might bear it. God had answered as He answered Paul—answered with a grace that was sufficient for Matheson's every need.

When first this burden was added to his blindness, it had seemed crushing. It was still there, but it was a different burden now. The light of a love that would not let him go had worked a transformation, and he could sing:

> "O Cross that liftest up my head,
> I dare not ask to fly from Thee:
> I lay in dust life's glory dead,
> And from the ground there blossoms red
> Life that shall endless be."

3

"Wonderful Words of Life"

A BRIDGE gave way as a train was speeding westward through Ohio, and in the wreck a well-known hymn writer lost his life. They took his baggage on to Chicago, where, when the trunk was opened, they found an unpublished song. In these words the soul of P. P. Bliss gave its message from the great beyond:

> Sing them over again to me,
> Wonderful words of Life;
> Let me more of their beauty see,
> Wonderful words of Life.
> Words of life and beauty
> Teach me faith and duty;
> Beautiful words, wonderful words,
> Wonderful words of Life.

For the Christian heart the old, old story has a wonderful attraction. We are as children in its presence. The child knows his favorite story so well that he eagerly corrects the slightest mistake in its telling, but still it holds the central place in his heart. Its charm is beyond the charm of others, and a suggestion of a new story often meets with an immediate objection and a request for the old favorite.

So the opening thought of the song is appropriate. The

more we know of Jesus, the greater is the joy in hearing words that tell of Him. The expressions of the old, old story may be familiar, but its appeal is forever new. Another hymn writer aptly says:

"I love to tell the story,
  For those who know it best
  Seem hungering and thirsting
  To hear it like the rest."

The thought changes. The words of Life call for more than personal acceptance, adoration, and prayer. They come with a challenge that will not be denied. Their song is a pæan of praise that must be sung where other ears can hear. Their joy finds permanent lodgment in the human heart only when it overflows to bring that joy into the life of another. The singer turns from what the story means to him to what it should mean to those around him, and he goes on with his song:

"Christ, the blessed One, gives to all
  Wonderful words of Life;
Sinner, list to their loving call,
  Wonderful words of Life.
All so freely given,
  Wooing us to Heaven:
Beautiful words, wonderful words,
  Wonderful words of Life."

Mr. Bliss had heard the echo of the voice that called to the burdened hearts of men, saying, "Come unto me, all ye that are heavy laden and I will give you rest." Hearing that call, it seemed natural that he should turn with a repetition of the invitation. As Andrew immediately sought to bring his brother to the Master, so Jesus expects those who have learned His love, to tell the story to those who need the comfort of its message and the power of its salvation.

The road to heaven is not intended to be traveled alone. The riches of Christian life are not for those who grasp with a miser's hand. If the message of Christ is worth accepting, it is worth passing on to bless the lives of other men. Even the great parting promise of the Master is based on this condition, for He says, "Go ye and teach all nations and lo, I am with you even to the end of the world."

The spirit of the stanza finds attractive illustration in a series of two pictures. In the first, a rugged rock surmounted by a cross rises from a stormy sea, and just beyond the reach of the waves a soul clings in safety to the foot of the cross. In the second, the same rock rises above the angry sea and the same soul clings to the foot of the cross, but now one arm encircles the cross while the other is extended to help another struggling soul to safety.

Henry van Dyke rightly says, "There is a loftier ambition than merely to stand high in the world. It is to stoop down and lift mankind a little higher." There is a higher joy than that of the self-centered life. It is the joy of knowing that our efforts have lifted the burden from the heart of a fellow man. Even the Rock of Ages seems dearer when we have found a safe place there for a soul brought to the foot of the cross through the touch of our hand.

The voice that was stilled still sang:

"Sweetly echo the gospel call,
　　Wonderful words of Life;
Offer pardon and peace to all,
　　Wonderful words of Life.
Jesus, only Savior,
　　Sanctify forever,
Beautiful words, wonderful words
　　Wonderful words of Life."

Its call is a challenge from the great beyond. As the words of Colonel M'Rae came from Flanders Field saying,

"To you from falling hands, we throw
The torch. Be yours to hold it high!"

so to us there comes the gently insistent call for a life that will echo the Gospel message and teach the nations of Him who gave Himself for us. The old, old story falls sweetly on ears in tune with the divine, but it needs the strength of consecrated Christian life to rebroadcast the message so that all men can hear.

4

"In the Garden"*

THERE is a significant suggestion in the fact that during the Exodus the children of Israel were directed to offer up a lamb in the morning and another in the evening.

To the average man it seems almost an accepted fact that evening is the time for prayer. It is then that problems, failures, and disappointments bear heavily on heart and soul. Pain and weariness tell of a need for strength greater than man's own. It seems natural that like a child, weary, disappointed, and in need of comfort, he should turn to his father at close of day.

Yet there is danger in this. Man needs to know God. He needs to commune with Him—not just tell Him his troubles. In the prayer of worry at eventide one is prone to give undue emphasis to his own affairs. A wonder as to whether he has done the right thing, a fear that his words may have wounded some soul, a feeling of the futility of the things accomplished—all these seem a crushing burden from which he must find release. So pressing are they at close of day that one may be tempted to think of them rather than of God. They may even crowd into the forefront of consciousness to such an extent that he is inclined

* Copyright by The Rodeheaver Hall-Mack Co., Winona Lake, Indiana. Quoted by permission.

to think of God in terms of His ability to meet these needs of the hour—to think of God in terms of what he can get God to do.

But prayer is more than asking for things. It is opening the doors of the heart so that God may come in and commune with man. To give a balance to spiritual life, to enable man to know God as friend and companion as well as comforter, another period is needed. It is the period of communion and friendship in which man begins the day with God.

Unless the day is bracketed by these two periods of prayer it is as a picture half-framed. He who has never crept into the shelter of the Everlasting Arms at close of day has yet to learn the fulness of our Father's love. Yet to think of God only as a shelter in time of storm, to call upon Him only when we see serious danger ahead is to yield to the temptation of the evening prayer—to think of Him in terms of what we can get Him to do.

To sit in quiet communion at His feet brings a richness of life unknown to those who call upon Him only in times of need. It would be unfair to the sisters of Bethany to say that one had a greater love for the Master or that one appreciated Him more than the other. It undoubtedly was Martha who sent for Him when her brother fell sick. It was Martha who hastened to meet the Savior while Mary sat at home too crushed to respond even when the Helper was nigh. Yet it was Martha who was rebuked because she allowed what she thought of as the needs of the hour to press so heavily that they left no time for communion with the Christ.

One responded with faith that Jesus could help and an appreciation of His care; the other, with an appreciation of His presence and a longing to be near Him. Martha loved Him for what He did, and served Him because of the things He had done; Mary loved Him for what He was, and sat in communion at His feet that her soul might absorb the joy and the power of His presence.

It is this spirit, the spirit of Mary, that finds expression in the opening words of the beautiful hymn of morning devotion by C. Austin Miles:

> "I come to the garden alone
> While the dew is still on the roses,
> And the voice I hear, falling on my ear
> The Son of God discloses."

If we are to think of prayer as opening the doors that the soul may commune with God the thought is appropriate. The morning itself seems a time of beginning again. The wounds of the past are at least somewhat soothed and the worries partly forgotten. The glow of the eastern sky seems filled, not only with the brightness of a new day, but also with the promise of better things to come.

Even the partly forgotten cares of yesterday add their bit to the spirit of the hour. They remind us of Him who helped us in time of trouble and who becomes doubly dear in hours of companionship, when worries and doubts have passed. In the evening hour He proved a refuge; in the morning He comes as a friend—a friend whose presence brings joy to the heart and inspiration to the soul.

In speaking of this often neglected hour of morning communion, Bishop Burnet brings a challenge from the days of our fathers. "In the days of our fathers," he says, "when a person came early to the door of his neighbor and desired to speak with the master of the house, it was as common a thing for the servants to tell him with freedom, 'My master is at prayer,' as it now is to say, 'my master is not up.'"

Even a more pertinent challenge is brought by the Wall Street Journal. It tells us, "What America needs more than railway extension, western irrigation, a low tariff, a bigger cotton crop and a larger wheat crop is a revival of religion. The kind that father and mother used to have. A religion that counted it good business to take time for family worship each morning right in the middle of the wheat harvest."

If we are to think of prayer as opening the heart doors that God may come in, the words of Spurgeon have an added significance. "This is the fittest time for intercourse with God," he said. "While the dew is on the grass, let grace drop upon the soul." For unworried communion that will open the doors for grace to come into the soul the morning hour has opportunities unknown to the harried hours at close of day.

Too often we wish that we might have had the opportunity of walking and talking with Jesus while the morning light was breaking on the shores of Galilee and forget the opportunities for communion with Him while the morning light is breaking on three hundred and sixty-five days of our year.

The pertinent thought in the song is found in the closing verses of the first stanza:

"And the voice I hear, falling on my ear,
    The Son of God discloses."

The morning hour gives a chance to know Him, to commune with Him as friend with friend—not just to tell Him our troubles.

There is also communion in this hour that lays a foundation for companionship throughout the day. A hymn writer in appreciation of this rejoices that

"Where cross the crowded ways of life,
    Where sound the cries of race and clan,
    Above the noise of selfish strife,
    We hear Thy voice, O Son of man!"

But it must not be forgotten that much of the ability to hear Him comes from association earlier in the day. If we cannot take time to become acquainted with the sound of His voice in the quiet hours of the morning, we cannot expect to recognize it when he speaks in the rush of the busy day. If we cannot take time for Him to reveal Himself in the early hours, we cannot expect to know Him in the noonday crowd.

"Conscience," says Uncle Eben, "am a still small voice, an' most ob the time it calls up the line am busy." Likewise amid the distractions of the day God ofttimes speaks and man knows it not. Just as the man who takes no time to hear the voice of conscience becomes deaf to its call, so the man who takes no time to commune with God cannot expect to recognize His voice when He speaks in the busy hours of the day. The voice of God may be audible, but it falls on such a man's ear as the voice of a stranger speaking to some one else. Says Bishop Cushman:

> "So I think I know the secret,
> Learned from many a troubled way;
> You must seek Him in the morning
> If you want Him through the day."

It is the true morning meditation, the meditation that is not allowed to degenerate into mental laziness or mere formality, that makes known the voice and the presence of the God who goes with man throughout the hours of the day.

But morning meditation is more than a communion in which God can reveal Himself. It is a joy—a transcendent, transforming joy. It is necessary to know this in order to appreciate the ecstasy found in the second stanza. "I did not know the world could be so beautiful," exclaimed a new convert. Knowing the joy of the Master's presence had cast a glow of radiance over all that was around—a glow that made it seem like a new world.

The beauty of the surroundings when Christ is near is suggested in the first stanza. Spurgeon, with all his ability for making clear and beautiful statements, said, "When the dew is on the grass, let grace drop upon the soul." With him it was a mere statement of time. With Mr. Miles there was an appreciation of the beauty of things when Christ is present that could find expression only in the words with which he opens his song:

> "I come to the garden alone
> While the dew is still on the roses."

For him there was a beauty in the grass but a greater beauty in the rose. Only roses made still brighter by morning jewels of sparkling dew seemed fit as a setting when Christ was there.

The real center of the picture is the Master Himself. Without Him there is nothing but a garden, whose beauties may become a thought setting and a basis for comparison. In the mind of the author it is He who is supreme in the beauty of the hour. It is He who is the fairest of ten thousand. Therefore, it seems natural that there should be a joyous, wholehearted response in which he should sing:

> "He speaks and the sound of His voice
> Is so sweet the birds hush their singing,
> And the melody, that He gave to me
> Within my heart is ringing."

There was no need for an audible voice from Heaven to say, "This is my beloved Son. Hear him." That voice had spoken—spoken in the morning hour—and had revealed the Christ in all His beauty.

As on the Mount of Transfiguration, so in the midst of the garden of prayer a voice calls lest man forget that Christ is to be served as well as adored. Neither of the sisters of Bethany had grasped the full significance of spiritual life. One thought in terms of communion and the other in terms of faith and service. It was only when the two became combined that the Master was able to bring His richest blessings to the hillside home.

The faith and service of Martha is just as vital as the communion of Mary. Life is incomplete for him who thinks only of talking with Christ in quiet places. Communion is necessary and the morning watch vital. From them come the inspiration, the vision, and the strength necessary for the tasks we face, but the day is not to be spent in the garden. For us, as well as for the disciples on the mount, there is work to be done. He who meets the Master in the garden of prayer must follow Him into the fields of service.

In a realization of this, the author continues his song:

> "I'd stay in the garden with Him,
> Tho' the night around me be falling,
> But He bids me go; thro' the voice of woe,
> His voice to me is calling."

It is impossible to catch the vision of the Christ in the morning hour and not hear His call to service in the heat of day. Man cannot walk with Him in the garden and refuse to follow Him into the walks of men. He who attempts to remain in the garden remains alone—alone in a garden without a Christ. He who would maintain communion with the Master throughout the day must come to Him alone in the morning hour and walk with Him as he goes out among men—walk in a fellowship both of communion and of service.

Hermits in the Middle Ages felt that if they could only withdraw to spend their time in contemplation and communion there would come into their lives a fulness of fellowship that could not be found if they walked with men. In this mistaken and selfish withdrawal they shut themselves off from the very thing they sought. They shut themselves off from Christ, for in the heat of the day He is to be found in the walks of men. Those who would follow Him must follow Him there.

Wherever that may be, there is joy. The fellowship of the morning is complete only as it brings a knowledge of His presence in the midst of the service of the day. It not only sends a man out with strength and inspiration; it sends him out to walk with Christ. When a man walks and works with Him there must be joy. It cannot be otherwise when He is there.

Therefore, the chorus which at first seemed fitted only to the first and second stanzas has an application to the message of the third as well.

> "And He walks with me, and He talks with me,
> And He tells me I am His own,
> And the joy we share as we tarry there,
> None other has ever known."

Whether it be an hour of tarrying in the garden or a walk of service among men, he who truly meets the Master in the morning hour has joy as he walks and works and talks with Him.

5

"Silent Night! Holy Night!"

BEAUTIFUL as is the music of many of our Christmas carols, we need to go beyond it to enter into the full significance and to grasp the beauties of the song. Much of the appeal of this carol is due to the fact that Mr. Mohr seems to have projected himself into the silence of that night and to have carried back with him a true appreciation of its meaning to the men of the world.

It was a dark day for the Jewish people. They reminded themselves of the glories of the promise to Abraham and looked back to talk of the good old days when God stretched out His hand to deliver His people and make of them a great nation. But their glories were glories of days gone by. They attempted to console themselves with the great things of the past and the promises of the prophets that a deliverer would come, but all about them was darkness as hopeless as the world has known.

Some men lived in luxury and others had less than the bare necessities of life. So great was the need of the people that Josephus tells us that the great number of unemployed in the country was one reason why Herod set 50,000 men to work on his building projects.

Rulers were not above murder, even of innocent babes,

if they thought their power was threatened. Examples of inhumanity and injustice abounded. There was oppression under the Roman government, but probably little more, if any more, than there would have been under one of their own, for men had not reached a point where they could govern for the good of the people.

Even worse than this was the fact that the people had lost their spiritual contact. Only a limited number really knew God, and those who spoke fearlessly for Him faced bitter persecution. The Sadducees were frankly worldly in the philosophy they had substituted for religion, and the Pharisees had gone so far in their formality that even the best of them were separated from the needs of the people. Large numbers of these so-called religious leaders were so completely separate from ordinary men in their spirit of self-righteousness that, as Christ Himself said, they bound heavy burdens on men's shoulders and refused to offer even one of their fingers to ease or remove them.

God had promised that he would not forget Zion, but men had turned away from Him. Formerly the children of Israel had found comfort in the declaration of the Psalmist that the needy should not be forgotten. Now they wondered if God still remembered His people. The land was doubly dark—dark in disappointment and dark in the gloom of a nation that had forgotten God.

The world was ready for the coming of the Christ in one way only—in the greatness of its need.

With a full realization of this, the writer seems to have caught the gleam of light in a dark world and to have begun his song:

> "Silent night! Holy night!
> All is dark, save the light
> Yonder, where they sweet vigils keep,
> O'er the babe who in silent sleep
> Rests in heavenly peace,
> Rests in heavenly peace."

In that manger lay the babe for whom the hearts of men were not ready and for whom there was no room in the inn. Dark indeed was the night when men had no place for Him who came to bring light into their darkness! A poor man whose heart had been made sympathetic through suffering evidently saw the need and offered the strangers the only accommodation he had—a manger filled with hay. Here in a stable, either in a cave on the outskirts of Bethlehem or, as is more likely, in an humble home, in a place adjoining that where the family slept, was born the One of whom the angels sing.

While in the better parts of town near-great spent the night with other near-great and the prosperous dined in the inn, He who was truly great came into the midst of humble men. It was God's testimony of His interest in the ordinary, every-day sort of men. His own Son had become one of them.

But here and there, hearts were ready to receive their King. Out on the rough hillside was a group of men, who, spending their days in the great out-of-doors, had found time to meditate on the things of God. As they gazed on the mysteries of the heavens the firmament showed His handiwork. They looked on the recurring cycle of life on the hillside and saw His hand there. Nature all around them kept them reminded that there must be a God.

Around the evening camp fire they had sung their songs of faith. On the high places of the open hillsides they had mused over messages handed down to them from he prophets. In the loneliness of their life they had come to know God. He did not seem distant as He did to others of their day and when He spoke, their ears were open to hear His message, for in hours of quiet meditation they had mused on the promise that a great deliverer was to come.

Nor was it difficult for them to realize that he might come from the common walks of life. Had not Israel's greatest and most beloved king come from their own humble group? Had not the prophet with one of the most flaming messages for God left his flocks that he might warn men and call them back to a following of the mighty Jehovah? Out on the hillside social distinctions became superficial. God had raised up great men from the common walks of life, and it was not difficult for them to believe that He could raise the great leader in the same way. To men thus prepared there came a glorious light; for them the angel spoke; of them the poet sang:

> "Silent night! Holy night!
> Darkness flies, all is light!
> Shepherds hear the angels sing,
> 'Alleluia! hail the King!
> Christ the Savior is born,
> Jesus the Savior is born.' "

Still, the proclamation of the angel held a new note,

even for the shepherds. They were not troubled by the scruples of men such as those of Nazareth who would not believe in Jesus because they thought of Him as the carpenter's son. They were not worried by the preconceived notions of their leaders that the great deliverer must come from some rich and powerful family. But the angel had proclaimed joy to all people. That was new to them.

Their nation had been thinking of the promised one as a Jewish messiah sent to deliver the Jewish people. They were the one hundred per cent nationalists of their day. A subject nation, with an economic system that had broken down and a religion that had lost the beauty and strength of its early application, though the words of Jehovah were written in the books of the nation, they still thought of themselves as *the people.* The boast of their leaders was that they were the children of Abraham. All others were foreigners. When in the years of his ministry a centurion came seeking help for his servant they condescendingly advised Jesus to give it because he had been friendly to the Jews. He had built them a synagogue.

There is no evidence that the shepherds were narrow like many of their nation, but this was something they simply had not thought of. They had failed to understand the greater significance of the Christmas message—failed to understand that it was a message of joy to the whole world. They had failed to realize that this is the Father's world and that the imaginary boundaries of nations are drawn by the hands of men, not by the hand of God.

As the shepherds stood in reverence beside the manger, God was speaking in another way to men who also were ready for the coming of the King. Of the coming of these men from afar the writer sings:

> "Silent night! Holy night!
> Guiding star, send thy light!
> See the Eastern wise men bring
> Gifts and homage to our King!
> Christ the Savior is born,
> Jesus the Savior is born."

God had made the message world-wide. From where these men came we do not know, but they were from regions beyond the eastern boundary of Palestine. The language they spoke is unimportant. They were seekers after God, and He had sent His star to guide them to the One in whom all men are brothers—in whom there is no East or West, no rich or poor, but in whom all are gathered together as one in the compass of His love.

From far distances they had brought their gifts—the best they had—gold, frankincense, and myrrh. It was a present fit for a king, but better far was the humble spirit with which these learned and rich men knelt by the side of Him whom God had sent. Greater far was the faith that sent them to a far country to accept as redeemer and king Him whom they found in humble surroundings.

The beauty of the story is that the wisdom of the world united with the unlettered meditation of the hillside in paying homage to the King. The wealth of the East joined with the poverty of a foreign land to bring Him tribute. And both were accepted; nay, more than that, both were welcome. In the ordinary court the wise men would have been admitted to the royal chamber and the shepherds left to stand in the street. In the court of the great King they became as one in the acceptance of Him whom God had sent, and both brought the highest tribute in the sight of the divine Father, the tribute of the heart.

The last stanza rightly begins with a prayer for light, or, rather, for renewed light. So many doubts and fears cast clouds over the heart of man and so many things vie for his attention that the Christ Child continually needs to be revealed to the soul. The seeking heart of the men of the East, the open mind of the shepherds, and a renewed knowledge of the coming of the King are necessary to follow Him.

The star of the East still shines, but to shed its radiance for mankind it must shine into the individual heart. Otherwise, it is only a bright point towards which men may look with a passing interest, or view through darkened glasses—a light that has no light for the dark recesses of the soul.

The echoes of the angel song come with an increasing clarity over two thousand years, but to bring the peace of which it tells it must find an echo in the individual heart. Its spirit and its message are complete only when it becomes a joyous part of men's lives. Otherwise, it remains as heavenly music played to tone-deaf men—wasted on hearts unwilling to listen and unable to understand.

The final stanza, which begins with a prayer, ends with an exhortation to join in the praise and in the worship of Him of whom the angels sang:

"Silent night! Holy night!
Wondrous Star, lend thy light!
With the angels let us sing
Alleluia to our King!
Christ the Savior is born!
Jesus the Savior is born!"

The closing lines are a fitting reiteration of the thought of the song,

"Christ the Savior is born,
Jesus the Savior is born!"

—born that man may know the power of His salvation and the joy of His presence, a power and a joy which even the angel carol could only suggest.

6

"The Ninety and Nine"

AFTER an unusually impressive service on the subject of the "Good Shepherd," Mr. Moody turned to Mr. Sankey with the question, "Have you a solo appropriate for this subject?" Sankey's first thought was of the Twenty-third Psalm, but he knew that if he began one of the Psalms it would be only a moment before every man in that Scottish congregation would be singing with him. He paused, for, somehow, he felt that he should bring this message in song alone. In his hesitation a voice seemed to say, "Sing the hymn you found on the train yesterday."

With a silent prayer, he placed a newspaper clipping on the organ and, improvising his accompaniment, he sang:

> "There were ninety and nine that safely lay
> In the shelter of the fold;
> But one was out on the hills away,
> Far off from the gates of gold,
> Away on the mountains wild and bare,
> Away from the tender shepherd's care."

As the melody died away a great sigh seemed to go up from the congregation, and Mr. Sankey knew that the message in song had reached their hearts. There was a personal touch that gave them a vision of the value of man in the sight of God. They had felt as never before the power of a love that would not let them go.

There was a contrast that forced itself home. They must have known the cry of the poet who bewailed the fact of man's inhumanity to man. In Jesus they saw One who valued man as His fellow men did not value him, and loved him with a love beyond their understanding.

Some decades before, Napoleon, in the discussion of a plan of campaign, was reminded that it would cost the lives of a million men. He drew himself up in pride. "What are the lives of a million men to a man like me?" he demanded. In the Man of Galilee they saw One who knew the value of a single man in the sight of God and held him dear.

Such a contrast could not fail to make an impression on their hearts. Even Napoleon in his later life recognized the difference and acknowledged the greatness of this love. "Cæsar, Charlemagne, and myself founded empires," he said. "But on what did we found them? On the power of arms, and today they are crumbled into dust. Jesus Christ founded an empire on love, and today thousands are bowing at His feet."

The parable of the lost sheep on which this song is based is God's answer to the man who thinks that no one cares. It is not difficult for man to think in terms of national movements or to see the importance of affairs when empires are involved, but too often he fails to realize the importance of the neighbor by his side. He becomes so wrapped up in what he calls big issues that he fails to see that movements are made of men and that no movement can become great until it meets the needs and helps in the solution of the problems of the individual man.

In the sight of Jesus it is the individual that is great. His ministry was the ministry of the personal touch. The most prized of His recorded sayings were given to a very small group, or to one or two persons only. His message is the message to the individual heart. When He speaks, He uses the pronoun "you" and usually in the singular number.

It is this personal touch that is the foundation of the songs we love to sing. Miss Clepane takes over His story of the single lost sheep and makes it the basis of her song. Paul Lawrence Dunbar, with a spirit of similar appreciation, gives a picture of the shepherd who sought a little black sheep and smiled "like dat lil' brack sheep wuz the onliest lamb he had." Margaret Sangster catches the vision and tells us that

> "Never a foolish little lamb,
>   Astray in the gloaming dim,
>   But the tender shepherd knoweth its name
>   And calleth it home to him."

The emphasis of these three writers is on the fact that Christ deals with the man—not with the multitude. His message is more than a general proclamation. It is an invitation to the individual. His search is a loving quest for the straggler who stands in need of His care. Man's comfort comes from the knowledge that the Master's words are meant for him.

The Shepherd Psalm gains much of its beauty from the

fact that it is written in the first person. It makes the psalm seem real. We cannot repeat it without feeling that it has something to do with us. Even that wonderful verse in the third chapter of John has a deeper meaning when we make it personal. God seems nearer when we can say, "God so loved me." For a full appreciation of the message of this song we need only to add that additional touch with which Paul Lawrence Dunbar closes his poem: "An'—dat lil' brack sheep—wuz—me!"

The hymn is a series of pictures. The scene shifts from the lonely sheep on the mountain side to an attempt to persuade the shepherd that its rescue is of no great importance.

> " 'Lord, Thou hast here Thy ninety and nine!
>   Are they not enough for Thee?'
> But the Shepherd made answer, 'This of mine
>   Has wandered away from me,
> And although the road be rough and steep
>   I go to the desert to find my sheep.' "

There were myriad hosts around the Father's throne, safe and joyous in the presence of the King. It was true that out in the world man was struggling alone under his burden of sorrow and sin, but he was a wanderer from God's presence and disobedient to His law. The hosts of heaven might say, and justly so, that by his disobedience man had forfeited his right to divine consideration.

Still, in the greatness of His love God called man His own. The angels might wonder that He would give so much, but in the tender heart of the great Shepherd there was room for but one thought: "One of mine has wandered away from me." With heart that faltered not in counting the cost, there was but one decision. It was the decision of love. The lost must be found.

> "But none of the ransomed ever knew
>   How deep were the waters crossed;
> Nor how dark was the night the Lord passed through
>   Ere he found His sheep that was lost.
> Out in the desert He heard its cry—
>   Sick and helpless and ready to die."

It is doubtful that we shall ever fully know the darkness of the night our Lord passed through. We speak of the greatness of His love, but forget that a capacity for love means a capacity for suffering, unless that love is met with an answering love. We think of His wonderful touch on the lives of men and forget the cry, "O Jerusalem, thou that killest the prophets, and stonest them which are sent unto thee, how often would I have gathered thy children together, even as a hen gathereth her chickens under her wings, and ye would not!" The "would not" was the cry of a breaking heart.

As children, we never knew the sacrifices our parents made in caring for us. We did not understand the greatness of the love that prompted them to think of their children before they thought of themselves. More important than this, we failed to realize that they did not think of these as sacrifices at all when they enriched the lives of those they loved and when they were met with an answering love.

So we, as children of the divine King, ofttimes fail to appreciate the greatness of His love and the heartbreaks He endured as part of the price of our redemption. Our experience has not been enough to teach us that when men refused to respond, the physical suffering was even surpassed by the heart pain. A sensitive and sympathetic nature, shut out of the lives it longs to help, finds the suffering intense.

When hearts respond, sacrifice becomes a joy. When the door is barred to the advance of love the burden becomes almost unbearable. It was this that made the load of the Savior so heavy. Mankind would not respond to His love and those who did follow were unable to meet it in its fullness.

He gave them warning of the price He expected to pay for their salvation, and they began to go away in such numbers that He turned to those closest to Him with the anxious question. "Would you also go away?" He stretched out His hand to heal ten lepers, and only one came back to thank Him. He took his chosen three to be with Him in the darkness of the garden, and in His hour of need they slept.

The bitter crown of life came at its close and found expression in the cry wrung from pallid lips on Calvary, "My God, my God, why hast thou forsaken me?" He had cut himself off from God for the sake of men, and those men had nailed Him to the cross. The end came even more quickly than they had expected, for the bitter sorrows of the lonely hour had caused the sensitive heart to break.

The questions of the fourth stanza bring to the heart

something of a realization of what it meant to Him to give
Himself for us:

> " 'Lord, whence are those blood drops all the way,
>   That mark out the mountain's track?'
> 'They were shed for one who had gone astray
>   Ere the shepherd could bring him back.'
> 'Lord, whence are Thy hands so rent and torn?'
>   'They are pierced tonight by many a thorn.' "

The glory of this Shepherd of ours is that He thought first
of His sheep. It mattered not that life was crowned with
thorns. It mattered not that the pathway was full of hardship and danger, or that it ended in the darkness of the
tomb. But it did matter that a sheep was lost.

Those who flung the taunts at Calvary spoke a greater
truth than they knew. He saved others, but Himself He
could not save. He could have turned aside from the suffering of Gethsemane and Calvary, but in doing this He
would have turned His face from the sons of men. He
could have spared Himself, but it would have meant that
man would have faced an eternal darkness. The choice
was before Him, and yet there was no choice. The greatness of His heart would not allow Him to save Himself
when it meant the loss of man's last hope of eternal welfare. The good Shepherd could not choose except to give
His life for the sheep.

The last stanza is a cry of triumph:

> "But all through the mountains, thunder riven,
>   And up from the rocky steep,
> There arose a glad cry to the gates of heaven,

'Rejoice! I have found my sheep!'
And the angels echoed around the throne,
'Rejoice, for the Lord brings back His own.'"

This is the crowning touch. Hardships are forgotten. Sorrows are no more. Blood drops are still to be seen on the lonely mountainside, but the soul of the Shepherd is filled with joy. Bitter experiences lie in the background, but in His heart there is room for but one thought: He has found his sheep.

The writer of the song has chosen well. It seems natural that she should picture the hosts of heaven joining in the glad hour, but to complete the beauty of the picture there is need for one more scene—an individual picture. Unless His love is met with an answering love in the hearts of men the beauty of the picture is lost and the loving sacrifice of the Shepherd becomes a tragedy. All is not well until we love Him who loved us and in love gave Himself for us.

7

"Follow On"

THERE is no suggestion of a spirit that would walk only in pleasant places as W. O. Cushing begins his song:

"Down in the valley with my Savior I would go,
  Where the flowers are blooming and the sweet waters flow;
  Ev'rywhere He leads me I would follow, follow on,
  Walking in His footsteps till the crown be won."

It is an expression of contented faith like that of a child who thinks nothing of the difficulties or the dangers ahead so long as it walks by its father's side.

There is no basis for a cynic's query, "Is that all he wants—just the pleasant things?" Expressions such as this are common among those who have known the joy of walking hand in hand with the Master.

A statement very similar to that of the author is made by another well-known hymn writer. One declares himself in the words, "Ev'rywhere He leads me I would follow, follow on." The other says simply, "If Jesus goes with me, I'll go anywhere." Both seem to have been thinking of the journey as one of joy because they were to travel in the company of the great friend.

Another example of the joy of a faith that knows Christ comes from the far East. Miss Goreh sees only the beautiful in life as she expresses the thoughts of her heart in a hymn of faith and fellowship. It had not been easy for her. Coming from a high-caste Indian family, it meant a complete loss of position when she became a follower of Christ. It meant the loss of family and the loss of friends. It meant social and economic ostracism. To the daily associations that mean so much to us she became a stranger. Friends, family, and all the things in ordinary life that we call dear were put aside. It would not seem strange if, like the children of Israel in the wilderness, she had begun to long for the things that had been left behind, but there is no suggestion of this in the words of her song. It is rather a spirit of joyous appreciation that finds expression as she sings:

> "In the secret of His presence how
>   my soul delights to hide!
> Oh, how precious are the lessons
>   that I learn at Jesus' side."

This is as it should be. If a Roman emperor could say to a courtier, "Why should you worry when Cæsar is your friend?" and that man be comforted, it would seem fitting that we should see life's pathway bordered with flowers when the King of kings says to us, "Fear not. I am with you."

Mr. Cushing tells us that this song came out of a longing to lay all at the feet of the Christ who had given His life for him. Knowing the life and teaching of Jesus, he knew that those who follow Jesus cannot expect to walk only in the pleasant places. He had learned life's lesson.

He had learned that life does not consist of the things with which we surround ourselves. Its comfort is not dependent on skies that are always cloudless. Its joy does not come from an absence of hardship or danger. In fact, the opposite is true. Nothing brings joy to the heart and a song to the lips more truly than known safety in the midst of evident danger or the touch of a friendly hand that transforms difficulties and dangers on the pathway into mere incidents of the journey. The confident song of faith comes from a knowledge that in the dark places there is joy and strength in the presence of the friend who is closer even than a brother.

Mr. Cushing's was not a joy that could exist only in the absence of hardship and sorrow. It was a joy that rose above them. The second stanza is a frank acknowledgement that difficulties and dangers must be encountered, but in thought it goes even beyond the statement, "If Jesus goes with me I'll go anywhere."

The writer knew Christ and the power of His presence. It was natural, therefore, that there should be no hesitation in his heart as he continued his song:

"Down in the valley with my Savior I would go,
Where the storms are sweeping and the dark waters flow;
With His hand to lead me I will never, never fear;
Danger cannot fright me if my Lord is near."

There was no illusion in the mind of Jesus and no uncertainty in the teaching He gave His disciples. He prophesied clearly that men would crucify Him and warned them that if they persecuted Him they would persecute His disciples also. He told them plainly that in the world they would have tribulation, but added, "Be of good cheer, I have overcome the world." This was His challenge for a faith that would enable them to walk with confidence in places where storms sweep and dark waters flow.

It was the knowledge of His presence that gave them comfort in the trying hour and courage in the time of danger; peace when men said there was no peace, and certainty when men said there was no certainty. It gave a joy that enabled the disciples to sing in the stocks of the inner prison, and a spirit that found reflection in the confidence that caused the hymn writer to say calmly, "Danger cannot fright me if my Lord is near."

The Twenty-third Psalm is not a song of pleasant pastures. It is a song of pastures made pleasant by the presence of the divine Shepherd. It is the testimony of one, who, in experiences as rough as the rugged and threatening hillsides of Palestine, had found that there was nothing to fear. His soul had known no want because there was One near at hand who supplied his every need. His was the joy of one who had found the peace of still waters, even though near by a dangerous stream was raging. He knew of the presence of deadly enemies, but still he knew the peace of security. His heart was untroubled, for his Shepherd was stronger than his enemies—so strong that even in the valley of the shadow of death He could inspire confidence.

The disciples' lives illustrate the joyous faith of our song.

They had gained strength to face dangers calmly because they knew Him whom they believed. They had learned more than to turn to Him when they were afraid; they had learned to trust Him and not be afraid. This is the highest test of faith—the test that can be met only when men follow closely wherever the Master leads.

With a full realization of these things the song continues:

"Down in the valley or upon the mountain steep,
Close beside my Savior would my soul ever keep;
He will lead me safely in the path that He has trod
Up to where they gather on the hills of God."

In this, as well as in the earlier stanzas, there is an expression more positive than that of the writer who said, "If Jesus goes with me I'll go anywhere." The difference in spirit is illustrated in a story of the Civil War. In the darkest days of that period a friend is said to have approached the president with the words, "I have been praying that the Lord will be on your side." The reply was characteristic. "I am not so much concerned about that," said Lincoln, "as I am in knowing that I am on the Lord's side." The heart of Mr. Cushing's song is found in the determination to follow wherever the Master may lead. There is no suggestion of a condition. His decision is to go with Jesus, not to ask Jesus to go with him.

In this there is joy and strength, for there are no bars to prevent the working of God's will. There are no reservations to keep Him at arm's length. For the soul that keeps close to Jesus there is a fellowship unknown to the one who prays that Jesus will keep close to him.

There is a confidence such as that which prompted the blind singer to write:

> "For I know, whate'er befall me,
> Jesus doeth all things well."

In the shadowy places man finds confidence in the knowledge of the nearness of the Master. He knows that He who endured the lonely darkness of Gethsemane and the agonizing gloom of Calvary will be with him in the lesser darkness that falls on his path. Wherever the footsteps of the Master lead, man can follow and not be afraid. He who walks in nearness to Christ walks in the companionship of Him who casts out fear. For him who keeps close beside the Savior the uncharted future holds no dread. His song is a song of joy, not because there are no difficulties or dangers, but because his Friend is greater than these. As long as He is there, there is no reason for fear.

8

"Tell Me the Old, Old Story"

MR. DOANE, who wrote the music for this song, was introduced to the words under impressive circumstances. As he sat in the International Convention of the Y. M. C. A. at Montreal in 1867, Major-Generàl Russell, then in command of the English forces during the Fenian excitement, rose, and with tears streaming down his bronzed cheeks, read the words of Miss Hankey's poem:

> "Tell me the old, old story
> Of unseen things above,
> Of Jesus and His glory,
> Of Jesus and His love.
> Tell me the story simply,
> As to a little child,
> For I am weak and weary
> And helpless and defiled."

The tears of the major-general added to the force of the message, and the poem has a power of its own. There is no prayer in song that touches the heart more deeply— touches it whether it be the heart of one who feels a need to know the Christ of that story or one who needs to be reminded of the Christ he knows.

It is possible that Major-General Russell was thinking of men under him who had faced the test and gone out into the great beyond without hope—men who had given their lives for a country in which it may be that no one had cared enough to tell the story so that it seemed real to them. It may be that he was thinking of others in his command who needed the friendly help of Jesus because their temptations were above the ordinary. No one who has not been a part of the life of an army camp knows the need for spiritual help there. Kipling was mild in stating the natural results when he said that "single men in barracks don't grow into plaster saints." It may be that the major-general was thinking of those men of his who had learned to know Christ but needed to be reminded of Him. Certainly there was a personal reaction as well, for there are but few messages with the breadth of appeal that is found in this song.

The strength of this appeal seems to be in its sincere acknowledgement of the need of the Savior. Men can understand that. There is an appeal and a power in the faultless one that cannot be denied. A sincere cry to Him finds a sympathetic echo in the hearts of men.

Even those not numbered among His followers give testimony to this fact. An illustration far more striking than the well-known tendency of men to call on Him in times of extreme need is found in the attitude of a man whose friend was facing a severe crisis. Although not a Christian himself, he wrote to call attention to the Christ in whom that friend believed. The things on which he had based his life seemed useless in the hour of trial, but in the story of the Savior whom he did not follow, he thought he saw help for his friend.

What the special reason was behind the song we do not know. The fourth stanza seems to indicate that Miss Hankey felt something had gained an undue influence in her life, just as for a time thoughts of an earthly kingdom kept the disciples from entering into the joy of the greater kingdom their Lord had come to establish. As so often happens with us, something evidently had taken her eyes off the Savior, and finding herself like the sturdy disciple who sank into the waves, she realized what that lapse of attention had meant.

It would seem to be almost a parallel case to that of Peter when he saw that so long as he had kept his eyes on the Master he had walked on the waters in safety. Miss Hankey had known the joy of His presence as she had walked closely by His side, and in another part of the long poem from which both songs are taken she expressed that joy in the words:

> "I love to tell the story
> Of unseen things above,
> Of Jesus and His glory,
> Of Jesus and His love.
> I love to tell the story
> Because I know 'tis true;
> It satisfies my longing
> As nothing else can do."

Now, when it seemed that the contact had been broken, there was a cry for the restoration of that fellowship—a plea for a retelling of the old, old story that would bring her back into touch with Him. It was a cry like that of David —a prayer that God would restore the joy of his salvation.

The song is unique in that while obviously it is a hymn of prayer, the prayer is not uttered. The actual wording is a plea for someone to tell the story of Jesus, but in the background is a realization of soul-need so great that the spirit of prayer pervades the thought. It is unique also in that it seems to picture equally well a penitent soul pleading for a restoration of the joy of Jesus' presence and a soul without God longing for his saving power. In either case there is a heart wrung with anguish, a soul prostrate before God and an anxious face lifted to cry, "Oh, won't someone tell me of Him. I need Him." It pictures our own need and links us in fellowship with those who cry, for we know that none can satisfy except Christ.

There is a plea that makes the wording suggestive:

> "Tell me the story simply,
> As to a little child."

When the heart is burdened, man finds no consolation in obtuse or complicated statements. His load is too heavy to weigh the values of possibilities and find comfort there. He needs something so simple that he can grasp it with the confidence of a child. A child cannot understand a philosophy, but it can understand one who loves. Intricate plans for life are beyond its grasp, but it can put its hand trustingly in the hand of a friend.

So when the heart is troubled, philosophies—even philosophies of Christian life—mean nothing to a man. What he needs is a friend, one who can understand, one whose touch can draw him back in time of temptation or lead him onward out of darkness. The simple story is the story for him. It helps to hear of the gentleness with which Christ reached out to the sick and the sinful. It helps to see how He found worried hearts and shared their burdens. It helps to be told of the love that led Him to give Himself for us.

With this thought the author turns to the second stanza:

"Tell me the story slowly,
That I may take it in—
That wonderful redemption,
God's remedy for sin.
Tell me the story often,
For I forget so soon;
The 'early dew' of morning
Has passed away at noon."

In this age of speed—radio, airplanes, streamlined trains, and predigested magazine articles—the stanza has a message for us. It still requires meditation to know God. Modern inventions have not reduced the time necessary to commune with Him. Speed may have its advantages in the superficial things of living, but in vital matters of the soul it brings confusion that tends to make eternal values unrecognizable and to cause men to pass them by unnoticed. The mind of man, slow moving in comparison with the infinite, must have time to grasp the meaning of Jesus' message and the beauty of His love.

Those who tell of the Christ need to remember that He Himself took three years to let His teaching sink into the minds of His most intimate followers. When the mind of man grapples even with the more easily comprehended things of the infinite, it requires meditation before they sink into the soul. "Be still and know that I am God," commanded our Lord. He cannot be comprehended in a passing glance.

The old, old story needs to be told simply in order that man may grasp it, slowly that he may take it in, repeated that he may see its increasing beauty and then repeated often lest he forget.

These, however, are but the mechanics of the telling. The real power is found in the spirit in which the story is told. Men cannot speak as if matters were of indifferent importance and expect them to be accepted as things of eternal value. The old, old story cannot be told with a "possibly" or a "perhaps." It must ring with conviction. It must be told as if it were vital—vital to the one who tells and vital to the one to whom it is told.

When he was called into account for preaching so earnestly in the temple Peter had but one answer to give: "There is none other name under heaven given among men, whereby we must be saved." To him it was of utmost importance. Men were lost. He had the secret of their salvation. He spoke with intense earnestness, for eternal life depended on it.

It is with a plea for this spirit that the song continues:

> "Tell me the story softly,
> With earnest tones and grave;
> Remember, I'm the sinner
> Whom Jesus came to save.
> Tell me the story always,
> If you would really be,
> In any time of trouble,
> A comforter to me."

Too often "the children of this world in their generations are wiser than the children of light." They lay such
an emphasis on the issues of their affairs that men take
them seriously. Even though the issues are of less than
eternal importance and even though they may be of doubtful value, their salesmen plead so earnestly that men are
led to invest the best they have.

If the enthusiasm that has gone into the promotion of
questionable mining stocks, imaginary oil wells, and city
lots in the midst of swamps. . . . The comparison leaves us
silent. We stand reproved in the presence of the earnestness
with which men promote business enterprises, both of the
wildcat and of the legitimate sort.

In public meetings we sing lustily, "I'm here on business
for my King"; in personal contacts with men who need
His message we speak with less conviction than has a
clerk trying to sell a shop-worn article in a bargain base-
ment. With humility we are forced to confess that our
Father's business has suffered because we have remained
silent or because we have spoken with hesitant lips. In telling the story lightly and with diffidence we have discounted
its value in the eyes of those whom Jesus came to save—
discounted it in the eyes of those for whom there is hope
in none other.

The plea continues with well-directed emphasis. The
thought turns from the need of a Savior to the need of a
Comforter. All is not attained when the Christ of the story
becomes the redeemer of the soul. Trials come, temptations
harass, and the heart is troubled. There is continual need
for those of us who know Him to "comfort them which

59 ⌒

are in any trouble by the comfort wherewith we ourselves are comforted."

It seems almost a cry of our own heart that finds expression in the last part of the stanza:

> "Tell me the story always,
> If you would really be
> In any time of trouble
> A comforter to me."

We, too, have stood alone in hours of trial—alone when within our hearts we felt that Christ could help but found it difficult to reach out to Him. Longing was intensified and loneliness doubled when no one came to say, "He can help you. I know He can, for He helped me." We cannot keep from thinking how much it would have meant if only someone had reached out to take our hand and place it in His.

The almost tragic cry ringing throughout the plea links our hearts with the heart of the singer. She seems to see herself back in the soul-struggle when she longed for someone to tell the story and no one came. She seems to feel that even when she called, they told it indifferently, and her heart cries out for a more ready, a more careful, and a more earnest telling of the words so vital to man.

Another thought now comes into the song. The need for Christ was there even before she realized it. It was not enough for someone to answer when she called. Someone was needed to tell the story of Christ before she knew there was need of Him—to tell it so that in His story she might see her need.

The first three stanzas plead for the telling of the story to meet known needs. In the fourth is the realization that she needed Christ before she knew it. Now that she knows Him, there is still need for telling His story so that it may call her back when other things assume an undue importance—call her back even before she knows she has allowed her eyes to turn away from Him.

With combined plea and prayer the song continues:

> "Tell me the same old story,
> When you have cause to fear
> That this world's empty glory
> Is costing me too dear.
> Yes, and when that world's glory
> *Is dawning on my soul,*
> Tell me the old, old story:
> 'Christ Jesus makes thee whole.' "

Behind the whole song is a spirit of prayer; within it a testimony that none other than Christ can satisfy; throughout it a plea that man should tell of Him. Annie Johnson Flint says:

> "Christ has no hands but our hands
> To do His work today;
> He has no feet but our feet
> To lead men in His way;
> He has not tongue but our tongues
> To tell men how He died;
> He has no help but our help
> To bring them to His side."*

* Copyright. Reprinted by permission, Evangelical Publishers, Toronto, Canada.

Into our hands God has given the key to unlock the storehouse of heaven and bring its riches to the hearts of men. To us is entrusted not only the beauties of the old, old story but also the hopes of the men for whom Christ died. Unless we tell His story there is none other to give them the words of life.

The Master's measure of responsibility is the measure of Andrew and the measure of Cain. Andrew first found his brother and brought him to Jesus. God preserved that story for us as a memorial of faithful service. "Am I my brother's keeper?" demanded Cain. His question was so far from what God expects of men that He did not even deign to answer.

9

*"I'll Go Where You Want Me To Go"**

WHEN Christ calls men to follow, He does not always indicate where He will lead. It is the part of faith to trust—to trust Him to lead in paths where the heart grows stronger, where passing joys are molded into lasting peace, and where the touch of His hand brings transformation to the soul.

It may seem that we are asked to sail under sealed orders, as men have been known to do in an emergency. There may be times when, like the soldier, we find it necessary to go forward not knowing what even the immediate future holds. But for us there is a difference. The soldier knows only that he is a part of some plan of the commanding officer and that he may be sacrificed to gain that end.

Ours is not an unquestioning obedience. We have a Christ whom we can trust. There is a vision from Calvary that removes hesitation. We cannot doubt the love that gave itself there. In the presence of such love we cannot ask querulously where He would have us go or complain that the path may be rough.

A realization of this seems to be built into the song of Mary Brown:

* Copyright by The Rodeheaver Hall-Mack Co., Winona Lake, Indiana. Quoted by permission.

"It may not be on the mountain's height,
   Or over the stormy sea;
It may not be at the battle's front
   My Lord will have need of me;
But if by a still, small voice He calls
   To paths I do not know,
I'll answer, dear Lord: with my hand in Thine
   I'll go where you want me to go."

That some of these paths may be difficult, is not the main consideration. Only those who face problems have the opportunity for growth. That some of them lead through valleys of shadow should not be a deterrent. Even night has consolations when He is there, and joys that transform life draw their power from dark experiences that have gone before. It requires the play of light and shade to bring out beauty in human life just as truly as it does on a painter's canvas.

Wherever He leads there will be difficulties. The path to greatness lies through the midst of these. The soul that would know man and appreciate God must follow there. A prerequisite for helping the one and for serving the other is a willingness to walk in the paths of sorrow where both have trod. We cannot expect to follow God and walk only in paths that we choose.

This song is often thought of as the song of those who hear the call to distant places. The possibility is there, but it is not predominant. The real emphasis is placed on a willingness to follow where He leads—to go where He wants us to go, to do what He wants us to do, and to be what He wants us to be.

Instinctively, the author points out the temptation to think only in terms of the far-away. The opening words are clear:

> "It may not be on the mountain's height,
>   Or over the stormy sea;
> It may not be at the battle's front
>   My Lord will have need of me."

There is glamor in thinking of standing on some great height or in dreaming of honor to be gained at the forefront of the fray. We smile at the bubbling ambition of the boy who wants to march at the head of the procession proudly beating a bass drum—the bigger the drum, the better the honor. We know from experience the situation on the playground: "If you don't let me be pitcher you can't play with my ball."

This spirit is not confined to the days of childhood. More than one application has been dropped in the waste basket because the man, as he considered it, was asking for work suitable to his training and position. He was not willing to do the work that needed to be done. In this respect, we are not blameless in Christian life and outlook. At times we close our eyes to work about us and imagine ourselves as leaders of some great movement. In rosy dreams of what we would like to do we overlook opportunities for service in the things God has given us to do.

In the fond imagination of picturing ourselves as swaying great crowds we forget that the Master stopped to talk with a woman at the well, paused to heal a blind beggar by the roadside, and turned to call a despised publican

65

down from a tree. In thinking of brilliant things we could say before multitudes we overlook the fact that the most prized sayings of Christ were spoken to a single individual and under circumstances entirely lacking in glamor—spoken to a woman of unsavory reputation as she rested her water jar at the side of the well and to a man who came to talk with Him under the cover of darkness.

The tempting call of the exalted and the distant fell on the ears of the disciples also. Even Judas was willing to follow wherever the weary footsteps of the Master might lead, so long as in imagination he could see himself standing in the place of honor as financial secretary of a great kingdom.

The others disputed as to who would be greatest in the coming kingdom to such an extent that Jesus was forced to set a child in their midst as an example. "You do not understand," was the thought of His message. "You have been seeking high places for yourselves. Unless you change your attitude and become like a little child in simple faith and unselfish service you cannot even enter that kingdom." They still failed to see the greatness of the call to ordinary service, and on the last evening of His life He was forced to give another lesson. He took the place of the lowest servant and washed their feet. "Surely," we can imagine Him saying, "if I have performed this lowly service for you, you can forget your striving for high positions and serve wherever there is need."

The temptation of these things is real. Men are willing to undergo hardships in order to secure places of honor. The test comes in being willing to give the best one has in unspectacular every-day affairs. Too often in dreaming of distant greatness men let slip the opportunity for honored service and cling to honors no more substantial than the tinsel on a jester's crown.

Worse than that, they would advise God. They would tell Him where He could use them best, and become so wrapped up in ideas of greatness to be attained in the work of their own choosing that it would be with difficulty that He could use them at all. The author expresses an attitude necessary in Christian life when she says that even though it may not be in the spectacular walks, she will go wherever God wants her to go. All she asks is that He reach out His hand to lead her onward. Without such an attitude God finds it hard to use men either in their home community or in distant places.

The natural development of thought continues in the second stanza:

> "Perhaps today there are loving words
>   Which Jesus would have me speak;
> There may be now in the paths of sin,
>   Some wanderer whom I should seek.
> O Savior, if Thou wilt be my guide,
>   Though dark and rugged the way,
> My voice shall echo the message sweet,
>   I'll say what you want me to say."

The temptation to wait for what we call a more convenient time to speak for Him is as great as the tendency to dream of things in the far-away while we overlook opportunities at our very feet. Men face the challenge and console their conscience with a promise that they will speak when conditions are more propitious.

67

It is not easy to speak to friends about the intimate things of heart and soul. As a result, the weak hesitate and then remain silent. Those friends know us well and we know them. Probably it would have been easier for Moses to have responded to a call to organize a crusade in a foreign country than to go back to his own people. In sending him to his own, God gave him the most difficult of tests. Those people knew Moses—knew of his failure and knew of his rashness. On the other hand, he knew them—knew their lack of ideals, their lack of a common interest, and their lack of stability. It is no wonder he hesitated. It was the test of a tremendous task.

It is not easy to speak of higher things to those who know the intimate details of our life. A subtle and powerful temptation faces us. The little disagreements we have had, the unkind words we have spoken, the actions that were not in keeping with the spirit of Him whom we worship, assume threatening proportions. We hesitate lest our friend think of them rather than of what we have to say. Yet our challenge is often the challenge of the man of Gadara, "Go home to thy friends and tell them how great things the Lord hath done for thee." We cannot be true to Christ and tell only strangers of God.

> "Perhaps today there are loving words
>   Which Jesus would have me speak;
> There may be now in the paths of sin,
>   Some wanderer whom I should seek."

Our test is often the test of Andrew—the test of speaking to those close at hand. Andrew probably approached his brother with a trembling heart. He knew the bluntness of Peter and his impulsive temper, but he probably hesitated most of all because he knew that Peter understood the weaknesses of Andrew. The water of life was being transported in a clay vessel and the bearer hesitated because the vessel did not seem in keeping with the gift.

It was enough to make him pause. But the love for his brother and the appeal of his new-found friend prevailed. He told of Jesus and in that simple telling performed one of the greatest and most far-reaching acts of history. We do not hear much of Andrew, but countless thousands owe their salvation to the work of the brother whom he led to Christ.

It is no wonder that the author included a prayer in this stanza. Doubtless it was easy to recall times when there had been an urge to speak and temptation had whispered, "Wait," or fear had sealed her lips. Probably there had been times when there was need to tell some friend what Christ meant to her but the words had remained unsaid. The prayer of the song might well be written; "O Savior, to talk to those near at hand is hard—at times woefully hard, and I am afraid. Help me. Show me what to say and I will say it. I will speak today."

The song comes to a logical conclusion:

> "There's surely somewhere a lowly place
>   In earth's harvest field so wide,
> Where I may labor through life's short day
>   For Jesus the Crucified.
> So trusting my all unto Thy care,
>   I know Thou lovest me!

69

> I'll do Thy will with a heart sincere,
> I'll be what You want me to be."

In this the final word is spoken. It is a simple and unconditional statement of self-dedication. In it is the spirit of true greatness—the spirit God loves to honor, whether He calls to work near by or to lands far away.

The decision to do what He wants us to do is made complete in the resolve to be what He wants us to be. Either one without the other is of doubtful value. Taken together, they form a crowning glory in Christian service.

10

"Swing Low, Sweet Chariot"

THERE is a charm in the Negro spiritual that places it in a class by itself. Its logic may be lacking and its rhetoric at fault, but behind it and shining through it is the longing of a lonely heart, the joy of a simple nature, and the unquestioning faith of a childlike soul.

It is not a composition carefully worked out and polished. It is rather a collection of disconnected or loosely connected phrases harmoniously grouped around a central thought. The singer grasps some truth and with illogical spontaneity groups around this a collection of harmonious expressions. The harmony satisfies his musical ear while his heart finds comfort in the repetition of the one great thought.

The eye of the purely literary critic may find but little in this song to praise. Its expressions may seem too crude to satisfy his sense of the appropriate. Its organization is such that he may not think of it as a harmonious whole. But there is a heart-touch that makes it human. There is a faith that stirs the soul and a spirit that suggests a touch of the divine.

Judged according to our ordinary standards, it seems primitive. It is primitive, but in the simple trust there is a pervading faith that lifts the soul into realms of the sublime. At the sound of the sweet, weird refrain,

> "Swing low, sweet chariot
>   Coming for to carry me home,"

one can almost see dusky faces lifted up in the expectation that just as God's chariot came to carry His prophet home, so some miraculous deliverance will lift them up from the land of difficulty and bondage to the land of liberty and love.

Theirs was a hard lot. All about them men called their country the "Land of the Free" and yet held their fellow men in bondage. Even though in some cases it was only a river that separated the slaves from freedom it seemed an almost impassable barrier. Escape was difficult, and when possible it seldom could be attained except by the desertion of loved ones. With hearts filled with ineffable longing it was natural that they should turn their thoughts to that greater freedom when God should call them to His own land of liberty.

Such a longing found expression in the words of their song:

> "I looked over Jordan and what did I see,
>   Coming for to carry me home?
> A band of angels coming after me,
>   Coming for to carry me home."

When things seem difficult the first thought is that of escape. It is a trait common to human nature. Even the Psalmist longed for the wings of a dove that he might fly away and be at rest. Modern friends, knowing this tendency, have advised us that when the outlook is bad we should try the "uplook." This song is but the expression of earnest souls sincerely trying the uplook because for them the outlook held no promise.

Nor are they alone in this. Others also have found their comfort in a forward and an upward look. The same thought finds expression in one of our songs of a generation ago:

> "On Jordan's stormy banks I stand
> And cast a wishful eye
> To Canaan's fair and happy land,
> Where my possessions lie."

There is no fellowship like the fellowship of suffering. The slaves had watched beside each other in times of sickness. They had divided the bit they had in times of need. They had so shared the little joys and the big sorrows that they had come to think of themselves as a single band. Some of the more sanguinely courageous had even sent word by friends escaping across the river that they too would be coming at the first opportunity. So, when they thought of the journey to that greater land of freedom, it seemed only natural that they should sing:

> "If you get there before I do,
> Coming for to carry me home;
> Tell·all my friends I'm coming too,
> Coming for to carry me home."

With homes broken up and loved ones sold into distant parts of the country, it is not surprising that at times they

73

became discouraged. It is surprising to find such cheer in the midst of the conditions under which they lived. There may be a minor key in their music, but the marvel is that they could sing at all. It was faith alone that gave the vision of better things and divine hope that made the outlook possible.

Throughout the simple and somewhat illogical words of the song shines the light of transcendent faith, while the closing stanza is a clear expression of an unfaltering trust, regardless of what life has to offer. In the midst of the vicissitudes of life, in its joys and in its sorrows, the simple, trustful nature kept up its song:

> "I'm sometimes up and sometimes down,
>   Coming for to carry me home;
> But still my soul feels heavenly bound,
>   Coming for to carry me home."

They had learned the lesson Jesus tried to teach in that last talk with the disciples when He spoke to them in words that might be freely translated, "Whatever happens, hold on to your faith in God and hold on to your faith in me." In holding on to this faith the slaves found a comfort beyond any that man could give. One of the most serious indictments of their lot was the statement of one of their own number, "It takes away all the tomorrows." But through the power of this faith they were pressing on towards a tomorrow that no one could take away.

11

"It Is Well With My Soul"

FROM a rude hut in a leper colony there arose the tuneful words of the song:

"It is well, it is well with my soul."

As they fell on the ear of a passing stranger they took upon themselves a meaning above the ordinary, for their touch was deeper than that of mere music. They came as a testimony of transcendent faith in a place where the stranger would have least expected to find it.

He knew something of the problems of the unfortunates gathered there—the dark cloud cast over the whole life, the isolation that amounted to ostracism, the rigidity of existence that suggested imprisonment by bars more dreaded than those of iron. The sincere note of the song was the indication of a peace that enabled the heart to sing in surroundings where many were too crushed even to weep.

The song, one of the most beautiful expressions of hope for souls in dark places, came from the depths itself. In 1874 Mrs. Spafford and her four children were crossing to Europe, when the ship on which they were traveling collided with another in the mid-Atlantic and sank within a half hour. Knowing that the ship would sink, Mrs. Spafford gathered her children around her on deck. Together they knelt and prayed that they might be saved if that were possible, and that they might be willing to die if that were the will of God.

In a few minutes the vessel sank; they were cast into the sea and were separated. Mrs. Spafford was found floating in the water and taken into a boat, but all four of the children were lost. Immediately after landing in England she sent a cablegram to her husband, a Chicago lawyer, but the message was the heart-breaking words, "saved alone."

Mr. Moody who was holding meetings in Scotland at the time went south to try to comfort the bereaved parents, for as soon as he received the message, Mr. Spafford sailed for Liverpool. As he talked with them, Mr. Moody was pleased to find a spirit of trust that enabled them to say, "It is well; the will of God be done." It was suggestive of the faith of Job—the faith of a man who knew God so well that even in the darkest hours he held firmly to his belief in Him—the faith that in the midst of the bitterest of trials enabled him to say with conviction, "Though he slay me, yet will I trust him."

Henry van Dyke once said that nature grows her fairest flowers from ground that tears have made holy. His words are suggestive here, for the hymn of faith so dear to our hearts came out of this trial. Two years later Mr. Spafford wrote it in memory of his children. It was his testimony that God can sustain even in the darkest of dark places.

With this background, there is a deeper meaning in his words:

"When peace, like a river, attendeth my way,
    When sorrows like sea billows roll;
Whatever my lot, Thou hast taught me to say,
    'It is well, it is well with my soul.'"

These words are not to be taken as men sometimes take a testimony of faith—taken to mean that he was untouched by the experiences through which he had passed. There was an empty place in his life; there were recurring thoughts of what the children would have meant if they had been spared; there were moments of loneliness when he longed for that which was lost. Life had not dealt gently with him, and there were scars that could not be hidden.

To minimize his suffering is to weaken his testimony. In the beginning his was the faith of a man almost crushed —the faith of a man who could not understand, but who still held on to his God. With passing days, God spoke and the father's heart began to understand that even though he could not see clearly, God cared and all was well. Yet it is significant of the depths of his sorrow that, great as his faith was, it was two years before it found expression in the confident words of his song.

Men who complain of the bitterness of their lot need to know this. Faith untouched by suffering is but an empty word. It finds its fulness and its beauty in the midst of sorrow where there is none other to bring even a ray of brightness into a darkened life. Those whom God has sustained only in little things have only little for which to praise Him. Those who have never learned to walk by the touch of His hand when all was dark have never known that they can trust Him in all things. Those who feel that no one

77

has ever suffered as they have can find consolation in remembering that our great expressions of faith come from trials more severe than those of ordinary human experience. Strong faith comes only when men have learned that they can trust God in the dark places.

Bitter experiences in life leave scars on heart and soul just as injuries leave their marks on the body. No soul is untouched by its sorrow; every life bears scars from struggles through which it has passed. But those scars can bear a twofold testimony. They can remind man of the injury he has received and leave him feeling that no one has suffered as he has had to suffer; or they can stand as a glowing testimony of a healing power. It is only in the brightness of the coming kingdom that the scars will entirely disappear. In this world they remain to tell us of a grace that is sufficient for us. It is a testimony of God's power when the soul can smile through its tears. It is an indication of His presence when the smile of faith so transforms the heart that even the scars add to the beauty of life.

It takes the power of God to do this, but even that power is useless when man dwells only on the bitterness of his own experience. The hand reached out to heal the hearts of men bears the ragged scar of a Roman nail, but he who focuses his eyes only on his own hurt sees nothing of the testimony of love and understanding written there. He who looks only to self cannot see God. In the glare of the ever-present spotlight he keeps focused on his injury there appears nothing of beauty—nothing at all except the hurt. In the life of the man who even secretly blames God for allowing these things to happen the scars stand out in their

78

ugly contour and take for themselves the place God intended for the beautiful and the inspiring. In the soul of the man who trusts Him they stand in the transforming glow of a new life, and bear testimony that God can sustain even in the bitterest of trials.

Mr. Spafford wisely makes mention of times of joy and times of sorrow. Joys become doubled when God is there; sorrows lose their sting in His presence. However, the message is primarily for those who feel their burden too heavy to bear. It is his testimony that man need not bear it alone—that even in the bitterest experiences there is One whose grace is sufficient for every need.

The first stanza is Mr. Spafford's testimony that God had been with him. In the second he turns to the future with a spirit like that found in the declaration of the Psalmist: "Though I walk through the valley of the shadow of death I will fear no evil, for thou art with me." With quiet confidence he says:

"Though Satan should buffet, though trials should come,
 Let this blest assurance control,
 That Christ has regarded my helpless estate,
  And hath shed His own blood for my soul."

It was not easy to sing these words of confidence. It required the touch of God in a life surrendered to Him. The beginning of such a transforming faith is found in the knowledge that God cares for man. A reinforcement comes in the recognition that God has been with him in days of trial. The fulness of trust is reached only when man is willing to listen for the voice of the Father and ready

79

to bow in the prayer of the Savior, "Not my will but thine be done."

Such confidence is not for the man who is unwilling to walk where the Master leads. He who insists that God come and walk in the path he chooses cannot expect that path to lead upward to the hills of God.

His ways are higher than our ways, and man may not be able to see where they lead. But there is a strange paradox: when man looks forward with God he looks backward as well. Instead of seeing only the part of the road that lies ahead, he sees it in its full perspective, and in plain view beside the path there stands an old rugged cross. There is consolation in this ever-present picture. Seeing it, man knows that he can trust God wherever He may lead. Trials may come and the road may be steep, but not so hard as the path that led to Calvary. There is no argument that can prevail against John 3:16. If "God so loved the world" we need not worry lest He fail us in our need. The farther stretches of the road may be enveloped in haze, but in the light of that cross it becomes a golden haze, in which faith bears testimony of God and of His love.

With the cross in view, it is not hard to utter as our own the words of M. G. Brainhard:

> "I would rather walk in the dark with God
>   Than go alone in the light;
> I would rather walk with Him by faith
>   Than walk alone by sight."

Trusting Him in unknown paths is better than trusting ourselves in paths we think we know. With Him we may not know the path, but we do know the Guide. Reaching out with that other follower of His, we can say with confidence:

> "I do not ask my cross to understand,
>   My way to see—
> Better in darkness just to feel Thy hand,
>   And follow Thee."

He could not sing his song of confidence inspired by a vision of the cross without looking beyond and finding the greatest song of joy. The cross was God's remedy for sin, and no more was needed. In a realization of its sufficiency in meeting this, the darkest of all the experiences of man, Mr. Spafford sang:

> "My sin—the bliss of this glorious thought—
>   My sin—not in part but the whole,
> Is nailed to the cross and I bear it no more,
>   Praise the Lord, praise the Lord, O my soul!"

It was the supreme reason for rejoicing. With Peter he knew that there is none other name under heaven given among men, whereby man can be saved, and the bearer of that name was his friend. It was natural that his song should become one of praise. An earthly friend might help in ordinary trials, but in this God alone could bring peace to the soul.

The confidence of heart expressed in the first stanza was unshaken. Mr. Spafford knew Him whom he had believed, and he was fully persuaded that he was able to keep that which he had entrusted unto Him against the great day. His was a growing expression of faith, but he knew that the day of fulfillment had not come. He was still seeing as through a glass—darkly. Faith told him that all was well but that all had not yet been made perfect. His thoughts turned to the time when faith would be justified and joy complete in the presence of the King.

A suggestive picture comes at the close of the Revelation. The venerable John bows his head and prays, "Come, Lord Jesus," and, with a similar spirit, Mr. Spafford ends his song.

> "And, Lord, haste the day when faith shall be sight,
>   The clouds be rolled back as a scroll,
> The trump shall resound and the Lord shall descend,
>   'Even so'—it is well with my soul."

12

*"The Old Rugged Cross"**

IT is impossible to sing the songs of the Christ without singing of the cross. When man comes into personal touch with Him he comes into its shadow. To know Christ is to know that He suffered and to know that He gave Himself for the salvation of mankind. To know Him is to know the meaning and something of the measure of the sacrifice on Calvary's tree.

Nor is man's knowledge complete until it becomes more than mere factual understanding. It requires the response of the heart and the dedication of the life before he can say that he really knows Christ. The fulness of such a response seems to find expression in the spirit and in the words with which Rev. George Bennard begins his well-known song:

"On a hill far away stood an old rugged cross,
    The emblem of suffering and shame;
And I love that old cross where the dearest and best
    For a world of lost sinners was slain."

Distance, whether measured in terms of miles or in terms of years, throws a glamor and an atmosphere of beautiful

* Copyright by The Rodeheaver Hall-Mack Co., Winona Lake, Indiana. Quoted by permission.

suggestion over the hard facts of life. I have looked across the valley at rugged mountain heights and gazed in admiration. Far below the summit lay heaps of eternal snow. The glacier, with irresistible though imperceptible motion, crept downward towards the valley. The great peaks reared themselves far too high for plants to grow and were far too harsh and barren for man or animal to live. But still I gazed and wondered. The barren rocks took upon themselves a rugged dignity and grandeur that was in no way perceptible to the venturesome climber facing their cold and dangerous slopes.

Likewise, as from the vantage point of years we look across to that mountain height on which stood an old rugged cross it, too, seems clothed in rugged dignity and grandeur. The painters have thrown a halo around its summit. They have so represented it that we see the beauty of divine love pictured there but fail to recognize the horror, the suffering, and the shame. We must see these if we are to know the greatness of its message and the depths of its love, for it is the hard facts of the cross that bring us to a real knowledge that "God so loved the world. . . ."

The climber drawing near to the cold, icy rocks of the mountain side sees them in their harsh perspective, and we, drawing near the cross, begin to open our eyes to hard facts we scarcely thought were there. With a more understanding gaze we see the body of the Savior so beaten and exhausted that it falls beneath the weight of the cross. We shudder at the tremors of pain as roughly hammered nails are forced through the tender flesh of hands and feet. We listen as those pallid lips utter words of encouragement for those who love and prayers for the forgiveness of those who hate—and our hearts are filled with wonder. The meaning of the cross becomes more clear. No more does it seem a distant scene enacted on a hill far away and in a time long gone by. We see it as the crowning experience of One who loved us more than He loved Himself.

The hard facts of the cross become still more hard. Those for whom Jesus is giving Himself, those for whom He has just prayed, still remain to taunt and jeer. It becomes more than heart can bear. The lips so silent in physical suffering cry out in agony, "My God, my God why hast thou forsaken me?" The head droops and the loving, heroic spirit passes out. The suffering and the shame of the cross have done their work. It is not a pleasant picture, but those who would know how much Christ cared for them must find their answer there.

A thought that makes the message even more dear finds expression in the second stanza:

> "Oh, that old rugged cross so despised by the world
>   Has a wondrous attraction for me,
> For the dear Lamb of God left His glory above
>   To bear it to dark Calvary."

Ernest Renan in his apostrophe to Jesus cries, "At the price of a few hours' suffering, which did not even reach Thy great soul, Thou hast brought the most complete immortality." But Renan is wrong—a thousand times wrong. It was a lifetime of sacrifice and suffering culminating in the great sacrifice on the cross. It left its mark on heart and soul through the tears shed over the suffering of fellow men, the utter weariness when He had spent Himself in their service, the agonized cry when they refused His loving ministrations, the blood drops of Gethsemane and the dark hours of Calvary.

It is not enough to remember the sacrifice and suffering alone. The great love does not shine forth in its glorious beauty until we see that all this was for a definite, conscious purpose. A painter has given his conception of the life and work of Jesus. The scene is the carpenter shop at Nazareth. The Savior pauses a moment in His work, and as He stretches out His tired arms, the sun shining through the open door cast His shadow as the shadow of a cross. During his active ministry tender words of warning to the disciples tell of the shadow as it continued to fall on His pathway. The marvel of it is in the love that kept Him steadily on, knowing the darkness of suffering and shame that awaited at the end. This seems even more wonderfully marvelous when, with Margaret Slatterly, we realize that He was "alone in a world that could not understand, was too busy to listen and too selfish to obey."

By turning aside, He would have missed Gethsemane and Calvary, but He would have missed man as well. He had come to bear the cross for the salvation of mankind, and the heart of the Savior could consider no respite for Himself if it had to be purchased at the cost of man's eternal welfare. The choice was a conscious one. The Savior's love would not let Him save Himself at the cost of others. The way of love was the way of the cross. There was no other way.

The third stanza has a message definitely for us:

> "In the old rugged cross, stained with blood so divine,
>   A wondrous beauty I see
> For 'twas on that old cross Jesus suffered and died
>   To pardon and sanctify me."

It is personal. The first stanza tells us that the dearest and best for a world of lost sinners was slain but it does not point us out as those for whom He died. The second says that the dear Lamb of God came to bear the cross to dark Calvary, but it is left for the third to bring the definite personal message that, "Jesus suffered and died to pardon and sanctify me."

For each one the Gospel has a message of love and hope just as definite and as distinct as any message of condemnation for the man who ignores and breaks God's law. Just as definite as were the words of the stern old prophet before Israel's king, so definite are these words of divine love, "Thou art the man for whom Jesus suffered and died." It makes the message personal—so personal that the heart surges within and the lips are moved to cry, as cried that man of yore:

> "While I view Thee, wounded, grieving,
>   Breathless on the accursèd tree—
> Lord, I feel myself believing
>   That Thou suffer'st thus for me."

The song continues with the only decision that is fitting:

> "To the old rugged cross I will ever be true,
>   Its shame and reproach gladly bear,
> Then He'll call me some day to my home far away,
>   Where His glory forever I'll share."

87

No other expression will meet the challenge of the cross. I can bring trophies to prove my love. I can bring tributes of service to show that I appreciate His sacrifice, but these are gifts of the hands. God calls for the gift of the heart. The only thing that will show a true response is life itself.

> "So I'll cherish the old rugged cross
> Till my trophies at last I lay down;
> I will cling to the old rugged cross,
> And exchange it some day for a crown."

But even in that glad day the greatest joy will come in knowing that Jesus bore the suffering of the cross that we might share in the glory of the crown.